Lost in the poems

There's a girl. A writer. Well, poet I shall say. This is a story all about her. The dreams she wanted to achieve the struggles she had and is going through the suffering she did all in silence. She had waned to fulfil dreams of hers along the way but had no motivation to do so, but if your reading this, she did it! This is only the start of her journey, you may relate to some of her story along the way. Why don't you read along?

Chapter 1

It's all about looks

the comparison look she holds as her sister walks by. Whishing shed looked the same. She struggles constantly with the looks she's given and personality she can't change. The mirrors view is always different.

Mirror image

Why isn't my image like yours?

The reflections from the same mirror,

But you perfect,

And I'm like this,

Tears roll down my face,

Forming a puddle,

Where is the beauty of mine?

Is it there?

is it just the mirror?

Or do I need to change,

Myself?

The struggle of looking I the mirror suffocates her. She goes on and on until it burns. The rolls won't go away. The feeling won't disappear into the darkness. She has tried everything to fix herself. Everything. She is lost. She is out of options. No matter what the challenge she is always willing to take the risk. No matter how much the workout burns. It is no time to give up.

Just like candle wax

I'm candle wax,

My insecurities burning me out,

Until they can't no more,

As time goes on I feel lower and lower,

My confidence shattering,

It's just like candle wax,

My body burning like a flame,

Melting my insides like candle wax,

The temperature drops,

The flame is blown out,

The candle wax stops.

The lack of self-confidence that's hidden behind the smile she shows, slowly getting the better of her. The burning sensation of her muscles after working out on no food. Then it goes black. Does it stay black?

Black

They see it asleep,

They see it at night,

Not me,

My vision goes black most days,

Not from the lids covering my eyes,

Or my hands,

The world tilting to the side,

Then it goes black,

They all say lack of food that's what makes life tilt and go black. She manages to stay conscious. Practice is key. What would she end up like if she didn't stop herself from falling to the ground? Will they notice? Will they laugh?

Do they notice?

Do they ever notice,

I do try,

I got achievements,

But no one noticed,

Do they ever notice,

O they don't,

So I gave up,

Then they noticed,

The mockery the made,

They do notice,

At times there not wanted too.

The hatred she has when people only notice the bad in her choices.it always happens to her. No one rarely sees the good in her and what she can do. So, she stopped. Now look who's unhappy. she got detentions. Arguments with family. Where's the win in her decisions?

Chapter 2

Everything is all over the place

The mess caused. the thoughts in her heads. The words she says. It's all a mess. All of it. A mental mess. Everything is a mess for her.

Life's a mess

Life is a mess,

Just like my head,

Everything is all over the place,

My words all mixed up,

The thoughts taking over,

Where's my place,

Where do I go next?

Life isn't a mess,

I am.

It's not just her thoughts that's all over the place. The trust she puts in others. Who knows who too trust, and what too trust. No one does. Everyone is untrustworthy to someone at some point. But everyone feels untrustworthy too her.

Trust

Can we really trust anyone?

No,

No we cannot,

I had tried,

I swear I did,

But it's not that easy,

Is It,

We can't trust anyone fully,

I wish I could,

But I just can't,

It's all about,

Trust.

She only struggles because of people's actions and what they choose to do with the trust she gives to them. She's always expected to trust someone by the click of a finger. It isn't that easy. When will she ever be understood? It isn't her fault. She's always being bossed around, do this and do that. Leave her alone. It's everyone. leave her alone. She's a puppet on strings

I was under your possession

What was I?

Your puppet?

I guess that's what you thought,

Well I wasn't,

But yet you still grabbed those strings,

As if you're in control,

I was under your possession,

Not anymore,

Your "spell" wore off,

I'm free.

She had always felt as if someone had got her under their control. she is trapped. as always. She's judged for who she is and told how to act. Well not anymore. She's not letting anyone walk all over her anymore.

Set me free

I'm trapped,

I didn't commit a crime,

But yet somehow I'm behind bars,

Well it's what it feels like,

I can't have any freedom,

Someone set me free,

As if I'm Rapunzel in a tower,

Set me free,

Someone please,

Set me free.

She thought they were the right one. Obviously they weren't. they lured her in giving her freedom, but in the end she was even more trapped then she was before. They were so sweet. At first, then they made her feel like a prisoner. Why? why did they do it?

You were so sweet

Sweet like candy,

They say,

I don't,

There's a two-way sugar coated door,

I guess I took the wrong one,

You were not sweet like candy,

You were the kid that rotted my teeth,

I did not like you,

I loved you,

You were so sweet,

As they said,

What changed?

What happened?

Why did you choose to rot?

You used to be,

So sweet.

She says everyone always acts sweets at first but then she gets to know them and she sees how they are and what they really think about her. She stayed in that friendship for a while. It was toxic. She didn't know if leaving was the best option. She could get hurt.

Manipulate

Manipulate me as you do,

When will you stop,

I tried standing my ground,

But manipulation is hard to beat,

How could they? She was so nice. She tried so hard, but they lied to her. Why would they do that. she didn't do anything to hurt them. She didn't mean to if she did. She just wants the best for everyone. Why does no one want the best for her? They say they do but they don't. the lied. She doesn't know what to do anymore. Everyone always lies to her.

What a liar

You lied to me,

You said you didn't,

But you did,

I trusted you,

But you let me down,

You lied to my face,

How could you,

You lied to me,

You said you didn't,

Yet you did?

I have proof,

Don't deny it,

You lied,

I trusted you,

You let me down,

You said it was the truth,

What a liar.

Why does everyone lie to her? She didn't deserve that. She doesn't know what is happening to her. She's given up. She needs to focus on more important things. Yet she can't. Everything has gone wrong.

Chapter 3

Something is wrong

Something is wrong. She doesn't know what it is yet. She always has anxiety attacks. She always feels dizzy. What could it be? Is she going crazy. She's constantly "hallucinating". Well maybe. She can never get to the end of the day. She can't even get her words out sometimes. He head is constantly over filled.

So much yet so little I have to say

I feel as if I'm going to burst with words,

But then I start to speak,

And it all goes,

As if I was imagining it,

All along,

My head spins with words,

But when I'm ready to use them,

The spinning stops,

Nothings there anymore,

I start to panic,

What if I'm going insane?

Is there something wrong with me?
I can't tell a single soul,

No one will understand.

she can't understand what's going on, so how will anyone else? If she speaks up she will be humiliated if no one gets her. Everyone will be laughing at her. The feeling of being alone hits. She will laugh with them, brushing it off, yet she will be crying on the inside. She promises each time too "brush it off" and "let it go" it never happens. Her hands start to shake her breath gets heavy.

Something is wrong! She can't see straight. It's a double vision. There's two of everything. She doesn't know what's happening. it's terrifying. She's in a class, what can she do? She was fine last lesson. Why now? Nothing happened. She was sat listening, now she can't focus. The ringing in her ears. The drowsiness hits. She tried to focus as long as she could.

Lessons

I'm fine,

It's a lesson,

What's the worst that could happen?

Panic builds up,

It always changes,

I was fine,

Now I'm a state,

I don't understand?

When will it stop?

She wants one single day without struggle. Is it so hard? There's no one for her to ask for help from. She's says she's "fine", is she? Well. She feels fine in herself, but somehow she ant cope in a double session. What's wrong with her. She can't figure it out so how will anyone else.

Am I ok?

Let me start by asking,

Am I ok?

Are you sure I'm ok?

I don't think I am,

I'm so different now,

As if I was changed,

By someone,

Or something,

I'm not myself anymore,

So where am I,

I waited so long to change,

But for the better,

Let me ask again,

Am I ok?

Are you sure?

I miss the old me so much,

Where did I go?

Is she ok? Is she really ok? No. no she is not. When will the old her return? Will she ever? She won't. She can't. Too much has been done to get to where she is. It was a struggle. She hates the new her, something is always wrong. Her looks. The way she feels. She's scared for the future, if she makes it that far. What's next?

Chapter 4

Is it always the simple shapes?

She's tried to explain its not her fault. Simple shapes are always going to be simple shapes. So what if there not so simple one time?

Shapes

There are so many,

Just as many as your personality's,

The points are sharp like your tone,

But yet you hide that in public,

Why so?

Show off your shapes,

It shouldn't be that hard.

The disappointment and disgust she has in people when they don't show off their true shapes and colours in public. Why do they do it too her? They act so sweet and innocent when there's others around. She doesn't know what to do. She keeps it all too herself. Who is there too tell? She bursts. People think she's going insane. She doesn't mean to look that way. She can't deal with all this stress. So she gets creative with her escape and draws shapes.

Were so creative.

Are we?

Drawing shapes into our arms,

They could last a lifetime,

Or just a few weeks,

However so,

Were different types of creative,

I don't show my creativeness,

You do.

Shapes are always different to one another, just like people. Everyone is different, why not show it off. She doesn't like showing it off, because people share the people will always stare and judge. It's not her fault. Is it really that big of a deal anyway?

Big of a deal

Is it really that bad?

it can't be,

I never meant for it to be,

I didn't do it for attention,

I was just struggling,

I'm sorry.

She's always sorry. She always has to be sorry. Everything is always her fault. It's like everyone is blaming her, for everything. Even if it's not always her fault.

Does anyone ever understand that she isn't making mistakes on purpose? Do they every understand when she asks a question she isn't trying to start an argument. She's afraid. Afraid of speaking to her mom about anything. She can't say anything without a fear of saying something "wrong". She doesn't know if she will get a second chance of forgiveness if she goes wrong. If she goes too far...

What about the second chance?

Where did it go?

did it disappear?

I gave it to you,

But it did not return,

So what about the second chance?

Don't leave yet please,

I need you here,

Repay me what I gave you,

Remember,

The second chance?

Everyone needs a second chance. Right? So will you give her one?

Something is wrong. Again. It's like something is always wrong. Horrible things were said to her. She doesn't know how to cope with things anymore. What is there to do? No matter what she does, it will be wrong. As always.

Choices

There's normally a right or wrong,

Not for me,

I can't win either way,

I can never win,

I just want a chance,

A chance to choose right,

Can it be possible?

Are choices ever right? Are shapes ever the same? Is anything ever the same, or is everything always different? She hates change. Why are they always changing? It's not fair.

Fair point

You've got a fair point,

But so do I,

Its not safe is your point,

But I was struggling,

That's mine,

I wish you'd understand,

Yes, you have a fair point,

But some are easier said than done.

Some fair points are easy to work with but yet some not so much. The points that are able to be worked with are told to late in the race, as she had already made and gone through with the choice of what to do.

No come back

Once you start,

It's hard to go back,

But you've got to do your part,

You've got this don't start to slack,

Follow your heart,

Your lack of effort is showing,

Don't let that happen,

Or I'll be going,

It's always like a pattern with you.

It was hard to go back to the old her, after she started, but does she need to go backwards? Why doesn't she just head on forward? It will be hard, but she will get through it. She can have a fresh start with life. A new chapter.

Chapter 5

What is love?

This is her point of view on love, but everyone has different ways of seeing love depending on their relationships right?

They came at her doorstep begging for her love. She answered the door ready to give them all she had. She started picking the pieces of her heart. She handed them the pieces, large and small, with a smile. They took them so caringly that she felt as if no treasure in the world held as much value as her heart. Seeing the love they gave made her ecstatic. When she asked for the pieces, they lit them all on fire, and so she watched her heart burn in front of her bare eyes... till all that were left were black ashes. They took hand fool's and put them in her pleading hands, she watched as the remains of her heart touched the floor, as if they never had any value, as if her love was nothing but a game too them. They looked at her with joyful eyes and a smile as she slowly began to breakdown. Their joy made her forget about her own sorrow. She felt like she'd burn her heart over a thousand times if it made them happy. That is love.

Love is nothing but a game

A game they say,

It's not a fair game,

They always cheat,

Then I always lose,

People say love is forever,

But a game always ends.

Love always comes to an end. No matter what happens along the way. People say they have met their soulmate but she has never met hers. She doesn't ned to rush though, she's only young and it will happen to end either way.

What is love?

Love is what you share,

Love is what you take,

Love is useless,

Love is useful,

Love is timewasting,

Love is worth time,

Love breaks people,

Love fixes people,

What really is love?

I guess only some will know.

Love isn't always as it seems. People split apart after some time, that's why she's not trying to find love anymore. It hurts it really does, one partner thinks everything is going great the other not so much.

Are we ok?

let me start with,

Are we ok,

Are you sure were ok?

I don't think we are,

Were so separate now,

As if it's a 2020 replay,

We're not locked away anymore,

So where are you?

I waited,

You never returned,

So let me ask again,

Are we ok?

I miss you so much,

So I hope were ok.

Is anyone ever ok? To be "ok" they have to have trust in that person. What happens when they break that trust? Does is all end, crumbling to pieces? No. they try and start over but her heart is shattered, it will never be the same again.

Love isn't just for non-family members. She has a family member who she loved dearly but broke her trust. They told her the truth. The thig they've been hiding all along. She wasn't ready for it yet. She said she was, but really deep down she wasn't. why did they hurt her? She loved them so much. She questions, did they ever love her?

Why are you hurting me?

I can't believe your hurting,

What did I do too you?

Yes, I hurt myself,

But I did not expect you too,

I'm a disappointment I know,

But I thought you loved me,

So why are you hurting me?
like I did to myself,

It's my responsibility,

Not yours,

So why would you ever hurt me?

She trusted them. They hurt her. Just one everyone else. Why so?

Chapter 6

The disappointment

She's the disappointment. She always has been and always will be. She feels like she's constantly told off. She's not good enough for anyone no matter how hard she tries.

Disappointment

Disappointment is a feeling of dissatisfied with something,

Disappointment can be expressed by the frowning of ones face,

Disappointment tastes like a dish gone to waste,

Disappointment smells like an old shoe,

Disappointment feels like rain dropping from one's umbrella,

Disappointment looks like a heart breaking into a million pieces,

Disappointment feels like your mind won't shut up,

Disappointment feels like losing someone or something,

Or even yourself.

She knows she's a disappointment. She knows she's a mess up. She knows the world would be no different without her. She knows. She knows. She knows. She doesn't need to be told all the time.

looking back

I look back now,

Realizing the disappointment id cause my younger self to feel,

The little girl with such big dreams,

Now a teen not thinking such things,

The little girl not a care about what others think,

Now a teen always on the brink,

The girl always so cheerful,

Now a teen constantly tearful,

That little girl was excited for what was ahead,

Now a teen wishing she was dead instead.

Why does she keep doing that to herself? She needs to stick to the present not look back at the past. It doesn't matter. She needs to listen to her heart not her head. Its messing with her, cut it out.

Repetitive thoughts

Disappointment, disappointment, disappointment,

Words I chant in my head daily,

As if I'm reciting lines,

Ware and smile,

Acting as if I'm ok,

When im really not,

Laugh at stupid jokes acting ok,

Even if I'm not,

The words chanting in my head,

Getting louder,

And louder,

Now they're screaming and me,

Every second,

Every hour,

Everyday,

Smile and act,

Hide behind the mask,

Even if its cracking with every chant repeated.

Life is about choice. She has so many choices to make.is she making the right one? She hopes for the best most of the time. She tends to be indecisive. That makes life harder, but if she doesn't make a choice nothing will change, which is good as she doesn't like change. Even if she hates being stuck in the same place too. The question is, will she make a choice? If so, is it the right one?

The right decision

Sometimes the decision is right,

Even if it's the hardest to make,

The right choice,

Is the hardest to make.

Yes, her decision was right one and safest but it doesn't feel as if it was for the best. She's hurting. She's hurting bad. She wants to be ok. She wants to stop but she just can't. she tried for everyone. But no matter what, she couldn't help, now she's more of a disappointment. She's sorry she really is sorry.

Chapter 7

Sorry

Is sorry always the answer? In her world, yes. She as picked up a habit of it. She didn't mean too. It was her fault. She was always being told she was wrong, even if she wasn't. even when she says sorry she feels as if she has to apologise again.

Sorry

Your right,

I should be sorry,

It's all my fault,

I should be sorry,

What have I done?

I didn't mean too,

I lost everyone,

I did this,

Not you,

I should be sorry,

You have a right to blame,

It's all my fault,

I'm sorry.

She wishes everyone could know how sorry she actually is. She I sorry if sometimes she doesn't make you feel appreciated. She's sorry for everything.

She's sure she hurt you, that she let herself get carried away by her own thoughts. She's sorry. It was foolish of her. She just wants them to be happy.

I truly apologies

I'm sorry,

I'm sorry for hurting you,

I'm sorry for the things I said that day,

The things I didn't mean to say,

I was mad at you,

Was,

I'm sorry I hurt your feelings,

And that I said I'd be there for you,

When I wasn't,

I was going to change,

I was,

I really was,

I'm so sorry.

It wasn't her fault that she burst. Yes, she knows that she says most things aren't her fault, but most of the time in the bigger picture it isn't. people stress her out throughout the day or week. She gets worked up which leads her to burst at whom ever does the littlest thing to get her to the point where she can't handle it no more. She bursts into rage and anger without waning too. She can't keep it under control. She lets it all out. She realises that it's all a matter of guilt. She feels guilty, and no one understands her.

Guilty

The guilt will eat you alive,

And it did,

It swallowed me hole,

bit me,

and left no crumbs,

the guilt consumed who I was,

the guilt caused me to leave the scars on my skin,

I don't know where to begin,

It felt like a sin,

An image covered into my mind,

It haunted me every night,

Reminding me I was the problem,

I watched myself lose my kindness,

That was more heart breaking than the guilt itself,

I was the villain,

I was in defeat,

I lay on the floor,

There I weep,

I coloured my surroundings in dark grey tones,

Convincing myself that's all I'm worth,

The guilt eating away,

Until you find yourself surrounded with blood on the floor,

And you couldn't take it anymore,

The guilt will eat you alive,

Seeping into your skin,

Making it difficult to survive,

Blaming yourself each and everyday,

The guilt will consume who you are,

How can we survive?

Its haunting her at night but also day. There was no escape. Every little action she did led her to no escape each time, the only temporary escape let her to bad additions.

Chapter 8

Bad addiction

The addiction

Your like alcohol,

You're like a cigarette,

You're my only escape,

It may only be temporary,

It may be bad for me,

But your addictive,

You're the addiction,

You're bad for me,

And I've only done it a couple of times,

It's not my fault,

Your,

The addiction.

She tried to get rid of you. She tried to stop. She found her escape. It ruined her, but it was fun. She could finally stop feeling. She did it more and more. Feeling the happiest she had ever felt, even if it was for a few brief moments.

She knew it was destroying her, but the things that are bad for you end up feeling the best after all.

The evening of pain

What really is pain?

pain is a stabbing feeling,

Especially in the heart,

Pain, it fractures you into,

Pieces like a puzzle,

People say it leaves after you taught it a lesson,

So why is mine still here,

So what really is pain?

Could her feeling of pain be different to others? S, she feels pain physical but that's nothing compared to her other sense of pain. The truth is she doesn't really want to die with the blades that harshly cuts through her skin. She just wants to feel something. As she looks at the thick red lines, blood gushing, head doubting, voice breaking. She felt nothing. Even when the blood kept on spilling. No one to stop her, nor hold her. She just wants all the suffering to end. The sky that had witnessed her scars that won't heal. The midnights that had seen her shattered heart that can't be fixed. The questions remain, "will they care?" for all the days she poured rain, she now feels empty like a can with significance value. For all the memories she's missed, for all the anger she's familiarised. For all the pain she remembered. For all the "what if" she questioned. For a moment she just wanted to forget that empty feeling that she keeps feeling., the feeling that gets her overwhelmed. She doesn't really want to die. She just wanted to be at piece and have a moment for her to stop the words running from her head. She just wants to feel herself, not just that empty feeling that is buried deep in her. She just wants to feel the pain physically, I just wanted to cry. The truth is, no matter how heavy she feels now, she hates how numb she is. It's the feeling of finding comfort I her own sadness. No matter how much she wants to let it all out, her eyes are too tierd.

Overwhelming

My mind is like a rough sea,

It is overwhelming ad drowning me,

I can't get any peace or rest,

It never stops,

I am always stressed,

Please,

Somebody save me from these thoughts,

I am in need of help,

Just a little of support,

But in the end I am here,

Still alone,

Surrounded by fear.

She's overwhelmed. She's masking it. Her thoughts are overtaking her.She has to escape. She knows she said she would stop and she tried she was just stuck in a cycle. A cycle that is never ending she isn't sure how to get out. She needs help, but doesn't want help. Is there anyone really? Her mom isn't really the type to talk too and her father well.

Chapter 9

Fatherly love

Was it ever there? If it was, where did it go? Where was he? Where was he when she told him he was family. Why didn't he turn up to her dance rehearsals? She only wanted his approval. When will he become the father she always wanted?

To the absent father

If I could put,

The hollow ache,

That haunts me,

Into words,

I'd tell you,

I miss the father you never were.

Why did he cause all of this stress for her? The promised gifts. The promised visits. Were they all lies? She waited for him. He never showed. Why so? They met up once. It wasn't good. She was 6! She was still a little girl. Why did he hurt her? She cried. And cried. Her friends always say "my dad this" and "my dad that". She never got the opportunity.

Waiting

Waiting is what gets me nervous,

Nothing distracting my brain,

Its time wasting,

It needs patience,

Something I don't have,

I hate waiting,

Especially for news,

Is it good?

Is it bad?

I guess we will have to wait and see.

She can't keep waiting around for everyone and everything anymore. She's tired of it. She wanted to know more. She found him. Oh the mistake she made. It was awful.

I found evil

A father's love,

Veiled is darkness deep,

A heart leaking,

Where scars eternally seep,

The melody of a song,

One so sweet,

Now a haunting echo,

A rhythm incomplete,

As a child,

I sought for love so true,

But your poison touch tainted all I once knew,

Like a symphony without it's guiding tune,

My heart leaked sorrow,

Under a bitter moon,

I your presence,

A furore storm would brew,

With each passing day,

My innocence withdrew.

He stole the innocence within her. He destroyed her. He was meant to be her hero, not the villain in her nightmares. She needed him. He was her family. Was she not good enough? Was anything she did ever good enough?

The vision

I watch fathers and their little girls walk by,

Watching them walk away,

The glistening in her eyes,

Like he's her best friend,

A part of me breaks,

Every time,

I hope they stay that way,

I hope they don't end up like we did,

I watch as they fade into the distance,

Holding hands,

Smiling, laughing,

I really do hope they stay that way and not,

End up like me.

She grew up. She learnt to understand. Not why he left. Not that it's not her fault, but that everything happens for a reason. She tried so hard. He couldn't change what happened. She gave up.

Chapter 10

The becoming of an Explosion!

It's the end of another week. She's exhausted. She has kept everything in and she can't hold the tears back no longer. She explodes. She can't control anything. She doesn't mean too be like this.

An explosion like fireworks

Boom,

I went off,

Boom,

And again,

Boom,

The last one?

Boom,

Well I thought,

My ears ring,

My heart races,

My head pounding,

My vision blurred,

Screams were the only sound I could hear,

Not from people,

It was all in my head,

Explosion like fireworks,

If only it was.

She's not a maniac. She's not a horrible, spoilt girl. She's just hurting. She keeps everything to herself for so long, it begins getting too much. The feeling of it all being her fault. Deep down she knows it's what she's going through that's causing this and she's not in charge of that.

She can't cope with the pain anymore. Can't they see what it's doing to her. Why won't they just take the pain away? She's falling apart. She's so tired by the end of the week. Someone get rid of it. She doesn't want to feel like this all the time.

Guilt

The red on my hands,

The danger away from bay,

What do I do,

I'll never know,

Guilt,

Why did I participate?

Why did I choose this path?

What do I do?

I'll never know…

The guilt she holds. For what? She doesn't even know why she is guilty, she just is. Its taking over. Should she be guilty? Why? What's next.

Any ideas?

what's next,

It's your choice,

I feel lost,

Do you not have any ideas?

are we stuck?

We need to get out,

We're running out of time,

3.

People say life is long. Is it really as long as seen? She's running out of time. 2. She doesn't know when it's going to end. 1.

Time

Time is precious,

Yet we take it for granted,

We're running out,

Yesterday I was 5,

Now I'm 14,

Where did it all go?

Be careful with time,

You don't know how longs left,

It could all end,

So,

Take your time.

Chapter 11

The new school year

Not again. The energy she lost last year. She can't do this again. When will it end? She can't go through this again. She's exhausted.

I don't know,

What's the answer?

I don't know,

What's next?

I don't know,

What do I do?

I don't know,

Where is everyone?

I don't know,

Do I know anything? She doesn't know what's going on at this point. She wants to know, but when she tries to find out or listen her head fills with fog. She has too much to think about. School just doesn't seem that important anymore.

It's the first full week of school. The new school year. Time flies. She's living in memories, now thinking of them. She's year 10! Its mental. It's all going to be over soon enough. She needs to pay attention otherwise. Will she do well?

The best of the best

Am I?

am I really the best of the best?

I don't think I am,

I don't think anyone does,

I try to be,

But I'm always beaten,

Why can no one see me trying?

Chapter 12

Touched

It hurts. It does. She didn't ask for it to happen. It just did. She hears him. She can see him. She feels him. Why is he still there? He was left behind. Wasn't he? Is he imaginary. Did it really happen? No one else saw it happen. So did it really happen? Is it all in her head?

Why me?

I can feel the ghosts of your handprints,

Like scars that that aren't showing,

But still hurt,

No one else can see them,

But I'll always know they were there,

You didn't ask to leave your mark,

But before I could stop you,

You did,

You will never know what it's like for shadows,

To loom over your body,

Suffocating its innocence,

I hope one day,

Someone takes something as important from you,

As you did me.

She said no. so why carry on. She said get off, but you continued. It happened in the moment for a minute, but in her head for a lifetime. A minute of contact but a lifetime of pain.

Stopped

You stopped touching me,

But I didn't stop feeling it,

You went on with your life,

While I still have scars,

I thought you would never do that,

While scrubbing off what you do,

You acted so sweet,

Hiding the dark secrets,

It was only for a minute,

But a lifetime of pain.

It hurts, and she tears up most nights since the day his hands were placed on her skin, took a breath into her ear and took the innocence within her throwing it in the bin. She continuously grieves for the girl she could have been, or the woman she would be if his touch never marked her skin.

Silence

I didn't dare tell,

Nor take a loud breath,

I laughed awkwardly,

I moved away saying no thank you,

He left me alone,

I left my mom's side,

He came back,

I stayed with my mom,

Silent I kept,

We left,

That was weeks ago,

I'm still silent.

She was touched. She was scared. She was silent. She still is. Silence is the answer. Just brush it off, get over it, don't tell anyone. The feeling sensation. The breath on her neck. Imagery blocking her eyesight. It's all there. Is it going to go? No. no is what she should have said. No, no, no, louder. She didn't. is it best to stay silent, or speak up? She chose silent. Will he know she spoke of him? Isn't he with her everywhere she goes? Creeping up behind her. She can run but he will always catch up. She wants him to leave but he wont.

The sickening truth

Anger builds up,

I now understand,

I can feel everything,

But nothing,

I hurt inside,

I don't know how else to feel,

I don't know how to react,

I never did,

Sometimes the truth hurts,

But this doesn't hurt,

It's a sickening feeling,

A feeling I hate,

One I never want again.

The anger inside of her builds up, then settling, but continues to build up, once again. It happens over and over. Like ice. It ca melt then freeze, over and over. She thought she could protect herself from a such thing. Yet she couldn't. is it possible for her to do so? She doesn't think so. Its already happened once maybe she won't be affected next time, if there is one.

Wounds

They're open,

Yet closed,

They're visible,

But they're not,

The wounds left on my arms,

He wounds left in my head,

They hurt,

They burn,

They leave me feeling nothing,

But feeling everything,

A sensation I've never felt before,

One I want to get rid of,

A sensation of feeling something,

But at the same time nothing,

I feel pain and burning,

But yet I'm empty.

She wants a sensation of feeling but not the one she's getting. She wants to feel a sense of happiness, not a sense of his touch. She should have made it more specific., but would anyone really expect that she'd wanted his touch back.

It's making me go insane

I'm going insane,

I don't know what to do,

I can't cope with this,

I'm trying my hardest,

I really am,

My head is spinning,

I'm losing my mind,

I want to go to bed,

Waking up a new person,

But every day I wake up,

The same,

They say,

New day fresh start,

Is it really.

Is it really a fresh start? Or are you just pushing your actual feelings down, so no one can see how upset you are. She doesn't believe in a new day fresh start. If she did she'd be crazy! Fresh start means putting things that happened behind you and let it go, but how can she put all of that behind her if it keeps coming back? The reflection with red handprints.

Constantly

My eyes a blood shot,

The lack of sleep,

The red handprints,

Permanently painted there,

The danger a distance away,

But the memory a blink away,

They're tattooed into my body,

No matter how much I scrub,

How much I try to get rid of them,

They will constantly be there,

Constantly.

Chapter 13

Used

She was used. She still feels as if she's being used. Being pushed around. Supplying for them, but when it comes to her needing them they edge away.

Extra part

Do I look like an extra part to you?

That one can just push around?

Make fun of?

Control?

It stops,

Now,

I'm not an extra part,

I'm one of the mains,

I won't live under yours obeys,

It leaves me seeing nothing but you in the mirror,

In need of myself,

Stop making me an extra part to use,

Make me a main part,

Like you,

Enjoy time with me,

Not controlling me.

Everyone she went to used her. She couldn't leave. She was to sucked in. she did everything for everyone, making everyone else happy while draining herself. Is that really how it is meant to work?

It hit me

I'm alone,

I'm replaceable,

I'm ear but far from death,

The thoughts in my head shortens my time left,

I could go when I choose,

Or go when the world chooses,

It all depends on fate,

I've been replaced,

I've been alone,

I've been in a near death situation,

Will death return.

She knows she has been and will be replaced. So why does it hurt so much? She's trying really hard but it's not good enough. Even if she does her best, it's never good enough. At guides she feels as if she's not good enough. At school she feels as if she's not good enough. Even at home. But dance? She feels worthy. She wants to be there all the time. She belongs. Dance may make her feel worthy but she's still shattered into little pieces and dance can't fix that by itself.

Shattered glass

It's laying there,

Glimpsing in my eyes,

Just one time I say,

I bleed out,

Regretting my decision,

But loving it too,

Im finally feeling something again,

But its pain,

I want to feel happy,

The glass is still there,

The flannel on my arms,

Tring to hold me together,

The glass is shattered,

Just,

Like,

Me…

She's falling apart. She's drained. As if her life is falling to pieces' day by day. Nothing seems to be going in the right direction. She puts everyone before her, but no one seems to think she does. She is trying her best but it's still not good enough.

Standards

They're too high,

I can't reach them,

I'm trying my best,

Just give me a break,

Everyone is stressing me out,

I'm on the edge,

I'm going to burst,

Lower your standards,

I'm not perfect.

She feels as if she's just seen as a failure, as if no one cares how she feels as if they know she'll go to any length for anyone and she wouldn't expect it back. No one ever really understands how she feels, but now were going to tell you.

Chapter 14

The passing of a loved one

It happened the unexpected happened. She choked, and choked. Death amongst her. Hovering over her. Following her like a shadow. Her airways blocked. Rushing to the vets. Save her. Save her. The words traveling around her head.

Save her

She's only 8,

She's my everything,

Save her,

Save her now,

It's not her time yet,

Keep her with me,

Do it now,

I know you can save her,

So do it,

Now,

Save her!

Don't just lay there it's not over yet. She needs her. 8 years own the drain. Not even one last goodbye.

It's over

I can't live without her,

She may only be a pet,

But she was my everything,

She made everything better,

So many years,

So many memories,

No more we can make,

But many I remember,

It's all over.

She left it on a bad note and couldn't even say sorry. It was Wednesday she wasn't home till 7. She had netball and dance. If only she'd gone home. She thinks it's all her fault. Is it? She had to be professional, she was at dance. She had to put a smile on her face. It's been 5 days and she still waits for her to come home. She doesn't want to believe it. It doesn't feel right. She can't process it. Did it really happen? Yes. Yes, it did. She has to understand that. There's no going back. No more cuddles, no more treats, no more time.

Time out

It's not the step,

It's not like that,

At all,

It's not "no phone",

It's not like that,

At all,

It's not "go to your room",

It's not like that,

At all,

It's not any of them,

Time out,

I need a break,

Time out,

I need time to process,

Time out,

I just need some,

Time out.

Let her have a break. Give her time to process things. She just needs space. She knows it's all over but yet she doesn't. she waits for her. She looks for her, but she isn't there. She will never be there. Ever again. It hurts. She just wants her back. She was her everything. 8 years. 8 hole years. All taken away by the click of a finger.

Click of a finger

Is it magic?

Not the kind where you become rich,

The kind witches use,

The kind hat comes to haunt you,

I work so hard,

Just for it to come back in my face,

I get everything on track,

And it fails,

I burst,

I break down,

It happens so fast,

Like someone,

Clicked their finger.

Her cats collar. The collar on her wrist. The collar showing her she's by her side no matter what. The collar. "The only thing left." She says it too herself, And too herself she speaks. The realization hits. The only thing left... why? Why did she not choose one last goodbye? She was stuck. She'd let someone down either way. She chose dance, keeping her mind occupied. She'd only let one person down then. If only she had chosen to say, one last goodbye.

One last time

If I had said goodbye,

The last goodbye,

The goodbye with no,

See you later,

Or even a,

See you soon,

It was just,

Goodbye...

Chapter 15

All about them

It's all about them and never about her. She isn't jealous, she's just alone. She just wanted something to be about her. It's never about her. It never will be about her. It's always about her sister. Her sister this, her sister that. Now its about her friend's daughter.

Just another

Once again I'm just another,

Not as important,

Not as pretty,

Not as smart,

I'm just another,

I don't mean anything,

I'm just here,

It's not about me

Its only about,

Them.

No matter how hard she can try she will never be good enough. She will never be as smart or as pretty as her sister. She isn't getting any younger so she isn't cute anymore. She's not an attention seeker she just wants to be recognised.

Tried to hard

I tried so hard,

No one noticed,

I tried so hard,

I became drained,

So I stopped,

Everyone noticed,

Everyone complained,

Everyone compared,

I'm stuck.

She's constantly told off for giving up. She gets it ok! She tried and tried but got

Nowhere. So what's the point of continuing to try? She's exhausted. She just

Wants someone to see what she's worth, if she' worth anything. She's so tired.

She's so drained.

Draining

It's all so draining,

I'm left empty,

Left with sorrow,

Left with questions,

I want the old me back,

The me that was left with,

Bubbles, excitement, enthusiasm,

not the one that is left with,

regret, questions, guilt.

She can't tell anyone that something is wrong, but she can tell you. Her head is

Constantly spinning. She bottles everything up making her feel sick to her

Stomach.

Sick to my stomach

I bottle everything up,

Feeling awful,

Stressed with only one way out,

I'm left in the dark,

No one to turn the light on,

Showing they care.

She has no one to tell her problems to. No one too share how she feels with.

No one to tell about how she feels disappointed, guilt, ugly after eating or the

Fact she wants to constantly cry over the feeling of a man ever minute of

Everyday. She can hardly sleep. Her sister hates her. Her sister is so horrid to

Her but when she retaliates she's the one in trouble. When will anyone notice

She needs help. She doesn't want it to be a big thing causing so much fuss she

Just wants someone to care.

She wants someone to make her feel she's worth something. Her mom

constantly complains how her sister has gone. She's 19? Is she not good

enough for her? Can someone just appreciate what she does? She couldn't

even have a moment on her birthday because everyone was making a fuss

over her sister. It hurts. When will anything be appreciated of her? People say

she should get her own money, or she should try harder. She's only 14 she

can't get a job, she tried, she put in effort but they never notice as it "wasn't

good enough". They say she's spoilt when it wasn't her fault her sister chose to

quit clubs. Once again she is 19 she should be paying for her own things

anyway. If the girl could do the same she would but she physically can't that's

why she asks her mom for things. Sorry she is not as pretty o funny as her

sister, even if she isn't that's no excuse to overlook her worth and not

appreciate what she can do and they can't?

imagine if none of this happened. Would she still feel this way?

sometimes just sometimes

sometimes I still think of the what ifs,

what if,

things had gone differently,

what if,

I didn't feel like this,

What would happen next?

What if I was more like my sister?

What if I made everyone proud?

It's a thought,

That devours me away,

But there's the horror,

In knowing,

They're only,

What ifs.

She feels like a third wheel no matter who she's with, but she feels like this

Mostly with her "friends". They used to tell each other everything, but now it's

As if she knows nothing. They all call but now he only cares about the call when

her friends are on there. They're all speaking together but yet they still private

message. Could it be about her? She says they can have their privacy of course,

but that also means she'd like hers. They tell each other their conversations

they have with her, and not expect her to question theirs. They were all so

close; now separating. They are closer together now. She gets it things change, but she didn't think so drastically in that quick of time. If her friend is upset its "his priority" to make sure she's ok. There was a miscommunication yet it's still Her fault. They say she has feeling and that she should consider them but she is Careful like she said, it was a miscommunication. They fix how one another feel But destroy how the girl feel. Did they consider how she feels? No, no they did Not. He friend was upset so he jumped to the gun thinking it was all her fault And was horrid to her. What happened? They used always to listen each other. Something dies inside her that day. What day you may ask; the day she found Out they didn't actually care about her much anymore. The day they made fun Of her. The day they, changed.

Chapter 16

Dizzy spell

It's been a week; it can stop now. Her head continues to spin. Reality not so real. Absorbed into her thoughts. Vision pixelated. She is going to bed but her stomach is sick. It's all in her head. Let her go. What has she been up too. She shouldn't be feeling this way. Snap out of it.

Snap out of it

My thoughts take over,

Swirling around,

Visions of pixels,

Real yet unreal,

Awake but asleep,

Zoned out,

Miles away,

No one had to know,

Sucked into reality,

But only when sat.

She sits and feels real. She stands, or walks and everything begins to feel like a dream again. Is she awake? Is she living quietly in a dream? Does everyone feel this way or is it just her? Should she speak to someone? Or would she be judged? It's the weekend. Sunday to be exact. 5 days after the incident. She's heading out to Nottingham. She fears for her chosen rides. What if it happens again? Is she prepared?

Prepared for me

Am I prepared?

are people prepared for me?

My mom says,

I have this,

And I have that,

And I need this,

Ad I need that,

It never ends,

The list continues,

Why is there so much wrong with me?

Are people prepared for this?

Am I even prepared,

For myself?

Well? Is she prepared for herself? She thought she was. Yet now her heads

Saying she's not. She had practised and practised but it wasn't enough,

Well anymore. She thought she knew herself. Does she? At all? She wants

someone by her side, someone she trusts. Someone who will keep her safe.

Just someone.

I want you by my side

I want you by my side,

So I don't feel alone again,

I need the person back,

The one they stole from me,

They were always so kind,

But now they've taken you,

Away from me,

I want you back,

I really do,

Stay by my side,

So I don't feel alone again,

Please come back.

She feels alone, as if no one would've helped her even if they could. She fell in

a matter of seconds. She would never expect them to know if they weren't

there, but an ask if she is ok afterwards would have been nice. But they didn't.

they just laughed. Not even some reassurance? They used to always check up

on each other, always have fun, never argue. Everything changed so much. Is

this why she feels like this?

Everything changed with them

I actually felt alone,

That I'm worth something,

I trusted them with everything,

As if they were different from the rest,

They were my home,

Everything was fine,

That is until it all,

Changed…

Chapter 17

Moved away

He came. They became friends. They grew close in just a few weeks, even days. Everything was going great! She made a new friend. It. may not seem like a big thing but she struggled with that, that's why she was so ecstatic about being hi friend.

All by myself

I started a convocation with him,

All by myself,

I gained his trust,

All by myself,

I made an amazing friend,

I did that,

All by myself.

She has someone she could trust, someone who trusted her. They talked daily. They became very close. She introduced him to her best friend. It was all going great. The hole year was fantastic! They stuck together like glue.

Sticky situation

I'm in a sticky situation,

It was all going great,

Is it now?

It doesn't feel right,

The room is getting tight,

It's very tense,

The walls start to close in,

Swallowing me hole…

She did expect this. He's moving. Not just is minutes away but 4 hole hours. That isn't fair. It wasn't how it was meant to be. They were meant to be Forever. It was the summer holiday. He moved. He visited regularly, but it wasn't the same. It was like he was still in the town but they knew he wasn't. it was fun while it lasted.

Just what I needed

As if things couldn't get worse,

They did,

This is so what I needed,

Why is this happening to me,

Do I deserve this?

Everything is going wrong,

My life is falling apart,

Bit by bit,

And I can't stop it,

I tried,

I just make things worse,

As always.

She thought they were all just friends. Just close friends. Turns out they're not. Her best friend is dating him. She's not jealous. Of course not. She is so happy for them but, she knows where it leads from here and it isn't great. She's putting on a brave face. His friend joined. There a 4 now.

The first week. Only the first week. Him, his friend and her friend all hang out. If it was just the two she'd get it, but it's not. it's the 3 of them. Shes obviously hurt. They said he had no idea his friend was going, but they did. That's what she was afraid of.

Afraid

I was afraid of this,

I still am,

He's the one I miss,

School is where it began,

But he's gone,

And so is she,

My last hope withdrawn,

We used to be a three,

Now it's only me,

The worst happened, they argued. She was alone. The people she'd ask for help were the people she needed help about. Bursting into tears without them knowing, one wold drop from her eye each time she hit send. Friends fight all the time, but not them. They were different. It wasn't how it was before...

good vs evil

why is it like this?

it shouldn't be,

who's good?

Who's evil?

It's like were at war,

I'm evil they say,

But weren't they the ones who let me?

So how am I evil?

They'd say it was all her fault, but how is it? She's got so much on and they're blaming her. How can it be all her fault? She wouldn't have known they were all hanging without her if they hadn't called. What about the time where her best friend wanted to go with other friends, and so did she but her best friend went to him and he starts having a go at her over text without even knowing her point of view, and all along they both had a misunderstanding. He still carried on at her even though they had both agreed about it.

I'm losing everyone

Where are they all heading?

I feel so lost,

They're so important to me,

But I'm losing them,

I'm trying my best,

But it's not good enough,

I'm trying to make everyone happy,

But I'm upsetting someone,

Why can't I make everyone happy?

I don't care if it drains me,

As long as everyone else is happy,

They deserve to be,

Right?

She doesn't know what to do. I was all great until he moved. Until she felt alone. She loves them so much, she would give them the world, but would they do the same? She would've said yes without hesitation before, but now she doesn't know the answer. She feels clueless, as if she doesn't know them anymore, like they're people she just met. She wants to go back to how she used to feel when she as with them. A sense of joy, a spark that lit up making her feel bubbly and happy. Where did that feeling go?

Where?

Where did the feeling go?

the feeling of joy,

excitement,

a feeling I got when I saw you,

the feeling when I had so much happiness,

when I couldn't stop smiling,

where did the feeling go?

I need it back,

I miss it,

I miss you,

I miss the old us,

I miss the old,

Me.

Is it really possible that one's she loved can make her lose her spark that quickly? Is it really that draining to keep her friendships gong? He moved away. He only comes for one person, and one person only. Not it's not her. Why couldn't he have just stayed? It could've been different. Possibly? If only she knew how it would've been if he stayed. If they were still as close as they used to be.

How we changed

Where did the old us go?

Were different now,

Why did it change,

Wasn't it already great?

And now,

Well,

It's different,

Why did you change us?

Why did they change? Was it not up to his standards? Was it too difficult for him to move away and let them call, message or book tickets? He's still their friend of course, but why'd he do that to the group? Well to her. Yes, him and her best friend are dating, but even just for five minutes? Five minutes her could spare to even say hi. The call day and night. Just five minutes. He can spare five minutes for his other friends so why no her? It's all going wrong. her life is falling apart.

Chapter 18

Everyone deserves

Happiness

Everyone deserves happiness, so she tries to make everyone happy, yet she's not. No matter how hard she tries she ends up disappointing someone. She just wants to make everyone happy and no one is listening. She wants things to be how they used to be. She wants everyone to be happy. She wants her friend and her to message how they used too. She wants them to be happy but she wants to be happy too. Yes, they're closer now but can't they just spare 10 minutes? They rush off after 2 minutes saying they're busy. Are they? They call nonstop. Can she be included in something? They couldn't even notice her trying to join in in the conversations or that she'd messaged. She always wants to make them happy but she's so drained by it. Everyone should be happy. Shouldn't they?

Key of life

The key of life is happiness,

Is it?
even if I seem happy,

I'm still exhausted,

Do I show it?

Of course not,

I need to put others first,

I'm rarely happy,

Yet I'm still living,

Is the key of life,

Really happiness?

Things used to roll smoothly between her and he friends. They don't know, but she's trying her hardest to make sure they get what they want yet it's still not the same. They talk to one another constantly. They go to on another asking to see how they are, all the time. She just wants to be a part of that again. It's as if they're slowly forgetting about her. She just wants to feel true happiness again. She's sat in tears as it hurts. She doesn't want to keep living this way. She wants it all to be ok, not just for her but for everyone. She was fine with making everyone happy, she still is. It's just, exhausting.

escaped

everyone deserves happiness,

yet I can't seem to find mine,

I'm not worth any less,

Do we have to get in an orderly line?

Am I at the back?

I search for my happiness,

Yet it's something that I lack,

My only escape into happiness,

Is going into a new world,

The world that's only temporary,

That leaves a feeling of emptiness,

That's my escape,

That I need to escape.

She can't seem to feel anything other than when she's in her own world. The thing is she doesn't want to have an escape to be happy. She wants to be happy in the word she was brought into not the world that leaves an after effect. An after effect she already had before. The feeling she was trying to leave all along.

Distorted reality

I sit as I head on in,

Into a reality like no other,

One of a kind,

All on my own,

I travel,

Into a distorted reality,

One like no other,

I escaped,

All on my own.

Why is it, she has to go alone? Why not with others, who make her happy? She can't help wanting to leave this world. It's a struggle. She tries, day by day, yet no one seems to notice or care. Everyone deserves happiness. Right?

Happy ever after

What is this?

A joke?

This is no fairy tale,

It's reality,

Everyone says it gets better,

Again,

It's no fairy tale,

It's all just struggles,

Then you rest in peace,

There's your,

Happy ever after.

Chapter 19

Struggles

What's going on? Why is she so ill? She doesn't want to feel like this. She wants to feel ok again. It's such a drastic change. She wants to have the ability to do things again.

Struggling

I'm struggling,

Can't you see that,

I'm struggling,

Why won't you help me?

I'm struggling,

I just want this feeling to end,

I'm struggling,

Just help me.

She struggles all alone, while her joy leaves her body taking the smiles she

wore with it. Her vision blurs as she enters a new world. She zones out,

burning her eyes as if she's crying. He chest is heavy causing her to panic.

Panicked

My hands begin to shake,

My eyes start to twitch,

I struggle with each breath I take,

My thoughts beginning to switch,

Reality not so real anymore.

She imagines what the world would be like if she had not had this happen. If

only she'd been fearless. The thought of death hits harder than the realisation

she has of messing her life up.

Thought overflow

My heads a storm,

And storms devastate,

But every time it overloads,

I hold my breath,

And bare the hurricane,

Repeating to myself,

One more chance,

One more breath,

Just one more,

And I'll fix it,

Until one day I can't,

Hold my breath anymore,

And my head is,

Half a stormy evening,

One tear stained night,

Two minutes,

Five seconds,

Away from breaking down,

Until I realize I can't fix it

No more.

She slowly starts to distance herself from everyone as the rage builds up. She feels fine, "it's the truth", If only it was. The ghost shade of her skin showing the illness she tried hiding inside.

Pointless

Is life pointless?

We're going to die either way,

We're brought into this world,

We learn things,

Live in a cycle,

Then die,

Have fun,

It's your last chance,

Because you and I,

We were born to die.

She's scared of death, yet she knows it can happen whenever. She feels as if she's already close to death. The feeling leaving her in a fright. She wants to die, yet not so much. She'll hurt the one's she loves. She knows time goes quickly, yet she feels as if she's stuck in time. Why?

Simulation

Are my feelings true?

Am I actually falling for you,

I feel insane,

Yet I'm trying to get into the right lane,

I'm tired every day,

In every way,

From sleep to school,

Even just getting out of bed,

Every day is a simulation,

Proceed with caution.

"Get me out of this system!"

Chapter 20

Forever ended?

Is it forever? Is it temporary? The empty feeling, she holds, causing her to distance. The sorry she gave with the meaning. The sorry she received that means nothing. She gave up. Why say something they don't mean? Repeatedly! How could you do such a thing.

What do you mean?

What do you mean by that?

How could you?

I have done everything,

Everything I could,

Apparently it's not good enough,

Was I ever good enough?

Did he ever really care about her, or even trust her in the first place? He said yes", but did he really? She had been his friend since he had arrived, yet he replaced her. He replaced her with her own best friend and left her behind. He left her in the dark. All alone. She trusted him. She believed him. He gained all of her trust, and lied. Throwing it all back at her.

Liar liar

You're a liar,

Liar liar,

Pants on fire,

I trusted you,

But you had to let me down,

You lied to me,

You're a big,

Fat,

LIAR.

How could he do such a thing? She only ever wanted the best for him. She would try so hard to make them all happy, no matter the cost. She would hand them anything. She trusted him with her life and he lied. He bluntly lied to her. How could he? Can she ever trust him again?

Best for the best

I give the best,

To the best,

I was the best,

Now she's the best,

I gave you everything,

We even got a matching ring,

Now you've hurt me like a bee sting,

I can't forgive you,

It sucks when we argue,

If only you knew,

My point of view.

When will he ever put effort in trying to see her point of view. When will he listen to what she has to say. He won't. that's the thing. He won't listen to what she has to say, so why bother? She just wants people to listen to the actual words coming out of her mouth. Is it really that hard?

Challenge

You up for a challenge?

Because I'll give you a challenge

I'm not a challenge,

But this friendship is a challenge,

Just listening to me seems like a challenge,

You really want to see a challenge,

Because I can show you a challenge!

It's not a huge ask to just listen to her. She listens to him. Even if she's struggling so much, she will still forever listen. Always. She will listen to anyone no matter what. She just wats to make everyone happy.

What are you listening too?

I'm listening to you,

Too all of your problems,

I'm listening to my thoughts,

My thoughts tell me listen to you,

Even if they spiral out of control,

I still listen to you.

He lives a distance away yet he seems to get in the way of everything. Why can't she just be friends with someone without them talking about her o hurting her.

The dark

It all happens in the dark,

It's all smiles and laughs in the light,

But when the lights off,

It all vanishes,

It's obvious,

Now that it's in

The light.

She knew something was going on but she doesn't want to say anything. That was until it got worse. They would message constantly. They would give one another "the look", she knew what it meant. They would tell one another things she wouldn't be able to know.

I know but I don't

I know what you're doing,

But I don't,

I know you want to get rid of me,

But I don't,

It may seem as if I don't know anything,

But I know more than enough.

They may think she doesn't notice, but she does. She learnt her lesson. She thought it would've been different. It was not. It was the same as any other one of her friendships. How could she be so stupid and fall for it all over again?

Fell in

I fell in,

Into your trap,

You lured me in,

Making me believe you,

You're a fake,

I trusted you,

I trusted,

You.

She really did trust them. She'd speak about them, about how happy she was to find someone like them. Everything was going great. Was...

Chapter 21

Missing?

Has she gone missing? Teachers running around looking for her. She isn't missing. She's still there. Just hidden away from everyone. Everything. No stress from class, no stress from teachers, no stress from anyone.

Worry

"Your worrying me",

I'm not trying too,

"were concerned about you",

Ok?
I don't care,

Can you just let me have some air?

Stop bothering me,

And leave me be.

It's only been three days since she had gone back to school after the first half term. She's already given up. She's missed seven lessons in three days! Everyone is mad at her, but she can't help it. If there wasn't so much pressure on her then she could possibly feel free. The amount of pressure that is put on her is starting to make her feel ill. She can't be "perfect", she isn't the best she knows that. She wants to do well but she has lost all energy and motivation to do so.

Pressure till it breaks

Add pressure,

I can handle it,

Add more,

I'll be fine,

Add more,

I can suck it up,

Add more,

I just want what's best for you,

Sure add more,

And more,

And more,

Ok ok that's enough,

"we need to add more",

The spark inside me,

Gone,

The smile hiding my feelings,

Gone,

I cracked,

I broke,

I'm sorry,

I tried handling the pressure,

But it got too much.

She tried so hard, so hard to make everything right. She didn't succeed. She's a failure, a complete failure. She can't do anything right.

What is right?

Right and,

Wrong,

You're either right,

Or wrong,

How'd you know,

What's right,

And wrong,

You don't,

That why I do everything,

Wrong.

How is she meant to keep going with confidence if she always gets things wrong? She has always been taught right and wrong. So she does the opposite when she's wrong so why is she still wrong. What's the point in her trying to be right anymore?

That's why

That's why I don't try,

That's why I go "missing",

That's why I don't care,

Because I'm still wrong,

Either way,

There's no right,

Only wrong.

Is that why he doesn't arrive to lessons she can't do? Is that why she goes missing from the crowds? Is it all too much? Don't yell at her it's not her fault. Yes, there's rules but think about it, if you were getting yelled at for things you could help or struggled with, you would be annoyed or stressed and want to find a place alone. Right?

Alone

I hate being alone,

Yet I love it,

If I don't feel safe,

But I do,

Why won't you leave me,

Alone,

I'm safe,

All alone.

Shouldn't they be grateful she's actually getting out of bed just to get to school. She's there why keep going on at her? Give her a break. Be grateful.

Be grateful

Be grateful I'm there,

Be grateful I'm polite,

Be grateful I tell the truth,

Be grateful I put a smile on my face,

Be grateful about my few efforts,

Be grateful,

Be grateful,

Be grateful,

Before you lose It all.

She doesn't have to fake it too make others happy. She doesn't have to go. She doesn't have to put any effort, but she does. All for them so stop pressuring her to do more. She tried and it wasn't good enough. It wasn't good enough for anyone. So they should stop complaining that she hadn't tried and that she's wasting their time missing lesson. They should've appreciated what she did instead of expected more.

Expectations

100% attendance,

Your target grade,

To be "perfect",

To be focused,

It's not that easy,

I'm not perfect,

Stop trying get me to be,

"perfect",

I'll never be perfect.

She's not "perfect". She's not a robot. She isn't going to be able to succeed all the time. So stop expecting it. She's tired. She's drained. She has no motivation to do anything. She's ill. She just wants to get better and to be "perfect", yet the stress isn't helping.

Are you ok?

Are you ok?

"How are you feeling?",

"Are you having a good day",

Why are you bombarding me with questions?

I'm going to say I'm fine,

Either way,

Like 'm wrong,

Either way.

She's doing awful, but she can't say that, she has to put others first. It's the rules. Others matter more than her. That's why she has a break in lesson, so she's prepared to be there when everyone else needs her.

The one who's needed

I'm needed,

But not for my purpose,

I'm needed,

But only for few,

I'm needed,

No I'm not,

I'm used.

Chapter 22

Hurt

'it's ok to miss someone that hurt you'

She's been hurt too many times. She thought she could put up with it now, but what she didn't know was that if it happened too much she'd break down.

In the dark

Am I scared of the dark?

Or what happens in it,

Some people know,

Some people don't,

Some are afraid,

Some aren't,

I know what happens,

And I'm afraid,

It always hurts the most,

When it comes to light...

No matter if it's in the dark, it will always come to light. No matter if it's behind her back, she will always find out. No matter how bad it hurts she will always forgive. She could not forgive him.

What's he really like?

he was supportive,

He cared,

He made an effort,

He didn't judge,

Thing changed,

She came along,

Everything went great,

He lost interest in her words,

He only supported her,

Not me,

I've been,

Forgotten.

He changed. He hurt her. More than anyone. He expected her to just put up with it. She didn't say anything, until it got worse. She said something causing everyone to be against her. It hurt. It hurt so bad. The went from talking every day to one conversation a week. She'd lost them.

Downgraded

1 conversation a week,

Is that all I get now,

Is that all I'm worth,

Is it a punishment?

Ouch,

That hurt,

Glad to see you care,

No conversations?

Fine,

Go off to her,

Were done,

Were finished.

She would talk to him all the time. He was her best friend. She wasn't his. He had his priority's. she was not one. The chose one another over her.

The road that leads to darkness

It was light,

It went dark,

Someone pulled the switch,

The road ended in the distance,

Where did it go?

Did I reach the end?

it's constantly dark,

did the road lead to darkness?

I followed,

It all went downhill.

Why did she choose to follow the road? It was the wrong path to take. Everything she worked for was thrown away. It was useless. She had worked so hard to achieve what she has, and she lost it all.

Why did you hurt me?

I thought we were friends,

Why did you change,

Yes, I bottle things up,

Yes, I'm mean to myself,

I didn't expect you to hurt me too,

I know I'm a disappointment,

Though I thought I was important to you,

So why are you hurting me,

I loved you,

I trusted you.

She told him everything and he left her. Her found someone better. That's now his priority. It hit deep. It hurt.

Get me out

I'm trapped,

Trapped in a cycle,

A cycle of your poison,

Your poison burns,

It burns more than a flame,

The flame list on my desk,

The desk I video called you on,

I kept going back,

Every time,

I forgave you,

But forgive,

No more.

Why does she always forgive? She will get hurt in the process. It's as if she doesn't learn the first time. She falls for the trick each time.

I was tricked

You tricked me,

Just like everyone else,

Can anyone be truthful?

That's all I ask,

But you lie,

You tricked me,

Just like everyone else,

How could you?

I trusted you.

She wanted him to be trustworthy. She'd be hurt if she lost him, and she did. He promised they'll be friends forever. He lied. He broke the promise. The promise they made effecting her the most. She misses him. But everything happens for a reason.

Broken promise

If somethings broken,

It'll never be the same again,

Like our promise,

You broke it,

Now I can't trust you the same,

Why'd you do it?

Chapter 23

False hope

They all gave her false hope. They got it into her head that she was good enough, that she could achieve wonderful things. They lied. She tried at first but she still failed. Constantly...

Good enough?

Is this good enough?

Am I good enough?

Why are your expectations so high?

Is the effort I put in good enough?

am I ever going to be good enough?

For you.

Why can't any of her decisions be good enough for them? She is trying extremely hard. She was doing the best she could. just give her time. She has so much going on, stop with all of the pressure your putting on her.

Pressure

Your putting way too much on me,

I'm trying,

Your putting way too much on me,

I'm tired,

Your putting way too much on me,

I give up,

Your expecting more than I can give,

I quit.

They tell her she can do things if she puts her mind to it, but she's been through this before and knows she can't. they constantly give her false hope. She is always trying to please them yet it seems impossible.

Please?

Please forgive me,

Please?

Please accept my apology,

Please?

Please stop yelling,

Please?

Please forgive me,

Please?

Why are they mad at her? She only tried to help. She gave them everything she had. Everything. Why couldn't they just appreciate all the effort? She wouldn't have tried if they hadn't given her false hope. It was their fault in the first place. Wasn't it? She knew she wouldn't have succeeded, she told them that, but they didn't listen. No one listened. It's as if she was set up to fail. To look like a fool. How could they?

Chapter 24

Becoming of the shadows

She's one of them. Walking behind. Hardly ever noticed. Walking by, yet they're all distracted. Distracted by each other. They walk along the path, talking and laughing, not with her. He isn't even aware of what they're talking about. She's a shadow.

Individual

Just me,

I'm an individual,

I'm alone,

I'm an individual,

No one understands me,

I'm an individual,

All of my friends are together,

So I'm left to be,

The individual.

They could leave her left there for minutes, even hours, and completely forget she was there. That's how "distracted" they can be. They never actually notice when she speaks up. They never notice when they leave her walking behind. Why can't she just be included.

Forgotten

She said she'd come back for me,

She didn't,

She said she'd always stick up for me,

She didn't,

She said she'd listen,

She didn't,

Why?

Am I only useful when everyone else has gone?

They didn't keep their word. She trusted them yet they messed with her. She only wanted to get noticed. She's blending in with the background.

Setting

Spoken but,

Goes unnoticed,

Seen,

Yet forgotten,

Checked on,

Yet already broken.

They always leave her to go unnoticed and forgotten when she's around, but it's as if they finally remember that she exists, yet only when a distance away. They can't go with her name unspoken when unseen. Even if her name isn't remembered when she's around.

Why only speak of her when she's not around? They speak the unspoken when the unspoken is unheard. They constantly hide things from her. They constantly talk about her. Is it good? Is it bad? Do they notice she feels this way?

Almost

I was almost the shadow,

Almost was time ago,

I became a shadow,

Will I remain?

One foot in,

One foot out,

The past hitting me like a thunderstorm,

Almost wiping me away,

I head back to the darkness,

You tend to come back sometimes,

Pulling me out into the sun,

To then throw me back in again,

Lightning and thunder,

Covering the screams,

From the pain you caused.

She will always live in their shadows, picking up the darkest parts of them, like a doll being built up of all their broken pieces that were left behind. This all happens while they sit happily lighting up one others day with the smiles on their faces, making each other laugh through the rough days. She will always be the final option. The one they glance over. No matter how hard she tried to fit in she will never bring the happiness and joy they bring one another. The worst part of it all is that they can't see any of it. They can't see the light they bring with each step she takes. They don't realise how bright they shine in this world full of darkness. Their light will always be brighter than hers. That's ok. She would rather be in the shadows and let them shine, then shine and watch them dim into the shadows.

Hidden hatred

"I like being I the shadows",

I fight battles no one knows they give me,

I win at games,

No one knows I play,

Gaining secret success,

I have secrets others believe don't exist,

I know their secrets,

Returning for my privacy,

Every moment in the dark my thoughts,

Being only heard by me,

In my mind,

Are both pearls of wisdom,

And serpents hidden away,

I've always needed to be the,

Best of the best,

Or worst of the worst,

By hiding away, I can make sure that,

Stays forever,

I have power,

That's disguised by a shadow.

The disguise all from a shadow. The picture of being hidden away. It's a choice not chosen. A decision not made. They chose the path she took. Purposely choosing the wrong one.

Chapter 25

Letting them go

Are they available? Is she available? Would the need her? Do they need her? Even if she was available? She gets it. She's a busy person, that's no excuse. She told them she can free up space. Why won't they listen? She can make time if they need her to, but they don't. they're fine and happy without her.

Free?

Are you free?

Are you free?

I've waited so long,

Are you free?

You say no,

But you're with her,

Are you free?

I'm aloud out,

Are you free?

She would always put effort into their friendship, but they didn't care. They'd only want each other. She had let them go. She cried typing the goodbye but it had to be done.

"Never speak about my friend like that again, especially when there's no need. One you weren't there for that moment. You can hate people that's fine, I understand not everyone can like everyone that's fair but you don't go to her saying things that are rude and unnecessary because of something that was a long time ago, that has also been dealt with. Don't think you know everything because you were not there. I hope It's clear I want nothing to do with you anymore. You had no right or reason to do what you did. I do not hate a person. I could never hate a person, only the choices a person has made. My friend (her), I'm hurt by the decision you made choosing him over me. It hurts, but I'm glad you made a decision to be happy, that makes me happy. It may hurt after I've lost a lot for you and put you first in a lot of situations, but that's ok. I'll always want you to put your priority's straight and in an order that makes you happy. My friend (him), I wish you the best for the years to come. I would like you not to contact me or my friends again. You promised you would never hurt me on a call we had, and you couldn't keep that promise but I forgive you. Both of you are so happy together and I'm so proud of you for being there for one another no matter the situation. you guys being together brings joy to both yourselves and I because of the smiles on your faces. I'd never want to ruin that. I may be hurting by being left behind but it's fine. I'll find my own path and take it. Goodbye and thank you."

It hurts her to read it over and over but she needs to get it into her system that it's over and that she chose him of her. Even if you put all of your energy into someone to make them happy there could always be someone better and moe important.

Ungrateful

That's what you are,

Ungrateful,

I gave you everything,

You were ungrateful,

I gave you the world,

You were ungrateful,

You complained,

You were ungrateful.

How could they have been so ungrateful? She handed them everything. They didn't care. They expected more, so they weren't happy. She'd become drained daily. All because of using al her energy for them.

Wasted energy

You're a waste of my energy,

I am exhausted,

You wasted my time,

I'm hurt,

You used me,

You threw me out,

Am I your trash?

I'm disappointed,

I wasted my energy,

For you.

She'd go day by day to far lengths to make them happy. Making sure she'd put them first, before anyone else. Before herself. She'd work so hard even if she went unnoticed. She couldn't carry on anymore. She had to let them go.

Chapter 26
the isolated cycle

She began to isolate herself from everyone. Hardly speaking, going under the school stairs or sitting alone at break and lunch. The smug look on their faces, seeing her all alone. She's all alone… No one to be close with. No one to look out for. No one to have her back.

Joined separately

Were joined,

Yet were not,

We always have one another's backs,

Yet we don't,

We always choose one another,

Yet we don't,

We'll be together forever,

Yet we aren't.

She said she'd love them forever. She promised, and she wasn't lying. She will forever love them. even if she isn't loved by them. They mean the world to her.

The world

The whole world,

You mean the whole world,

That's a big deal,

The whole world,

The entirety of it,

You meant the world,

Why leave it behind?

The world Is huge,

That's how much you meant to me,

Yet you left it behind.

They hurt the person that gave them everything she could. Now she's alone. Isolated. "she's different." She's the one that waits, while sat alone at breaks. The one who distanced herself from the rest. Everyone with their own groups while hers had disappeared from eye sight.

Eye see

I see how it is,

My emotions like bubbling fizz,

I rescued you,

And I'd do it again,

I watched you go,

It put me at a low,

But,

I loved you,

And I still do,

I watched as you faded from my eye sight,

It cut deeper than an animals bite,

But I forgave you,

And I still do.

She is hurt. She is mad, but somehow she can and will always forgive them. Always and forever. She's sat alone writing this story so you won't feel alone. the way she did.

She just wanted all of her pain to end. She felt like no one could understand. She felt that it was abnormal for someone to miss someone that hurt her. But it's not.

I Emily Fitzsimons wrote this book to tell you if u relate to any of these situations you are not alone and it gets better.

Printed in Great Britain
by Amazon

36473808R00056